LITTLE JAMIE
BOOK

What It's Like to Be...
Qué se siente al ser...

GEORGE LÓPEZ

**BY/POR
KAREN BUSH GIBSON**

**TRANSLATED BY/
TRADUCIDO POR
EIDA DE LA VEGA**

Mitchell Lane
PUBLISHERS

P.O. Box 196
Hockessin, Delaware 19707
Visit us on the web: www.mitchelllane.com
Comments? email us:
mitchelllane@mitchelllane.com

Mitchell Lane
PUBLISHERS

Copyright © 2012 by Mitchell Lane Publishers. All rights reserved. No part of this book may be reproduced without written permission from the publisher. Printed and bound in the United States of America.

Printing   1   2   3   4   5   6   7   8   9

A LITTLE JAMIE BOOK

What It's Like to Be . . .   Qué se siente al ser . . .

America Ferrera	América Ferrera
George López	George López
Jennifer López	Jennifer López
The Jonas Brothers	Los Hermanos Jonas
Kaká	Kaká
Mark Sánchez	Mark Sánchez
Marta Vieira	Marta Vieira
Miley Cyrus	Miley Cyrus
Pelé	Pelé
President Barack Obama	El presidente Barack Obama
Ryan Howard	Ryan Howard
Shakira	Shakira
Sonia Sotomayor	Sonia Sotomayor
Vladimir Guerrero	Vladimir Guerrero

Library of Congress Cataloging-in-Publication Data has been applied for.

eBook ISBN: 9781612281384

George López likes to make people laugh. He has
been a stand-up comedian since he was 18 years
old. For many years, he traveled from city
to city. He still travels, and he
also acts in television shows
and movies.

*A George López le gusta hacer reír a la gente.
Ha sido comediante desde los 18 años. Durante
muchos años, viajó de ciudad en ciudad.
Todavía viaja, y también actúa en películas
y programas de televisión.*

GEORGE

In 2006, George was honored with a star on the Hollywood Walk of Fame.

En el 2006, a George lo honraron con una estrella en el Paseo de la Fama en Hollywood.

George pretends to be one of the Kardashians at the Teen Choice Awards.

George imita a una de las hermanas Kardashian en los Premios Teen Choice.

When George started working, it was hard for Latinos to get jobs as comics or actors. Some people have asked him to play bad guys in movies. George doesn't want people to think that Latinos are bad guys, so he does not take these jobs.

Disney's Mad Hatter
El Sombrerero Loco de Disney

Cuando George empezó, era difícil que los latinos consiguieran trabajo como comediantes o actores. Tuvo ofertas para actuar como el malo de la película. George no quería que la gente pensara que los latinos eran malos, así que rechazó estos trabajos.

SANDRA BULLOCK

One night, an actress and producer named Sandra Bullock came to one of George's comedy shows. She thought he was very funny and wanted him to star in a television show. *The George Lopez Show* ran from 2002 to 2007 and won many awards. Reruns are still played on many channels, including Nickelodeon.

Una noche, una actriz y productora llamada Sandra Bullock fue a ver una de las actuaciones de George como comediante. Pensó que era muy gracioso y lo invitó a ser la estrella de un programa de televisión. The George Lopez Show se transmitió desde el 2002 hasta el 2007 y ganó muchos premios. Todavía lo pasan en muchos canales, incluido Nickelodeon.

The cast of *The George Lopez Show*

El elenco de The George Lopez Show

Ann and a wax statue of George

Ann y una estatua de cera de George

George met Ann Serrano in 1990, and they were married in September 1993. Three years later, their daughter, Mayan, was born.

George conoció a Ann Serrano en 1990, y se casaron en septiembre de 1993. Tres años más tarde, nació su hija Mayan.

Movie *Valentine's Day*

Película Día de San Valentín

ASHTON
KUTCHER

George has been in many movies. He likes to play different characters. He has played a teacher, mayor, FBI agent, and even a Chihuahua in *Beverly Hills Chihuahua*. He is also Grouchy Smurf in the 2011 movie *The Smurfs*.

George ha aparecido en muchas películas. Le gusta hacer personajes diferentes. Ha sido maestro, alcalde, agente del FBI e, incluso, un chihuahua en *Un chihuahua en Beverly Hills*. También hace la voz de Pitufo Gruñón (Grouchy Smurf) en la película *Los Pitufos (The Smurfs)*, que se estrena en el 2011.

Un chihuahua en
Beverly Hills 2

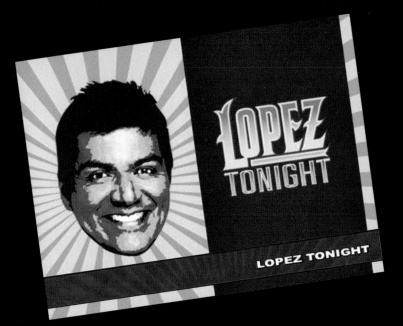

LOPEZ TONIGHT

George is the star and producer of another television show. Since 2009, his late-night talk show called *Lopez Tonight* has been on TBS. George works on the show Mondays through Wednesdays. He tells jokes and talks to famous actors, musicians, and sports stars.

George es el productor y protagonista de otro programa de televisión. Desde el 2009, tiene un programa de tertulia nocturno en el canal TBS, llamado Lopez Tonight. George trabaja en ese programa de lunes a miércoles. Cuenta chistes y conversa con actores, músicos y deportistas famosos.

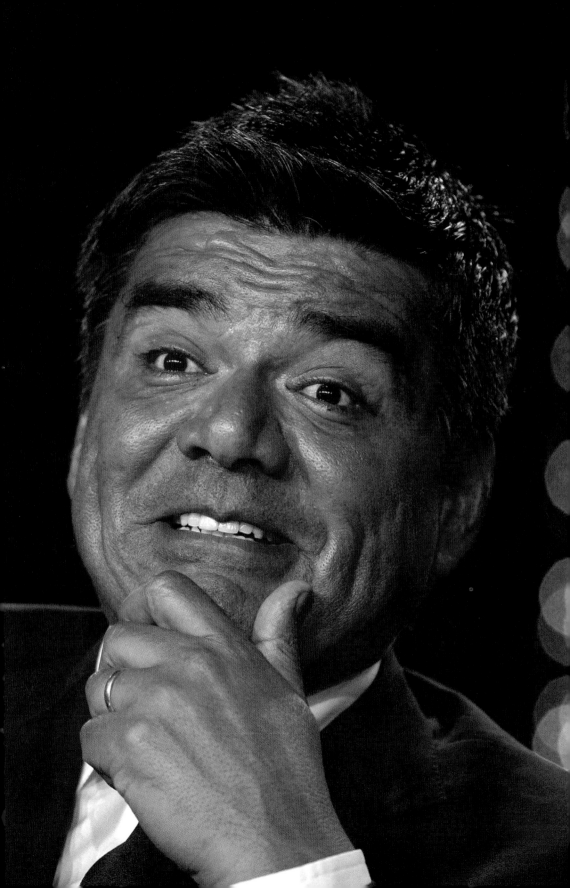

TYRA
BANKS

George with the Jonas Brothers

George con los Hermanos Jonas

George stays busy for the rest of the week. Sometimes he performs in comedy shows. Other times he appears on award shows. Two of his favorite award shows are the Nickelodeon Kids' Choice Awards and the Teen Choice Awards.

George se mantiene ocupado el resto de la semana. A veces actúa en programas cómicos. Otras veces, aparece en programas de entrega de premios. Dos de sus favoritos son los Premios Nickelodeon Kids' Choice y los Premios Teen Choice.

George and Ann started the Lopez Foundation to help people with kidney diseases and other health problems, and to raise money for schools. George also volunteers for the National Kidney Foundation. He helps other charities as well. One is PADRES Contra El Cáncer, which helps Latino children who have cancer.

George y Ann llevan la Fundación López para ayudar a la gente con enfermedades en los riñones y otros problemas de salud, y para recaudar dinero para las escuelas. George hace trabajo voluntario para la Fundación Nacional del Riñón. También ayuda a otras organizaciones benéficas. Una es PADRES Contra el Cáncer, que ayuda a niños latinos que tienen cáncer.

In 2005, George was sick. Doctors told him that he needed a new kidney. His wife, Ann, gave him one of hers. Now he is healthy.

En el 2005, George se enfermó. Los doctores le dijeron que necesitaba un nuevo riñón. Su esposa, Ann, le dio uno. Ahora George está saludable.

19

To honor Latino people in the United States, George spoke at the ALMA (American Latino Media Arts) Awards with his friend, Eva Longoria. He also went to Fiesta Latina, a concert at the White House that celebrated Hispanic music. George has been invited to the White House by two presidents, including Barack Obama.

George and Mary J. Blige sing with President and First Lady Obama.

George y Mary J. Blige cantan con el Presidente y la Primera Dama Obama.

Para homenajear a los latinos de Estados Unidos, George habló en los Premios ALMA (American Latino Media Awards) junto a su amiga, Eva Longoria. También asistió a Fiesta Latina, un concierto en la Casa Blanca que celebraba la música hispana. Dos presidentes, incluido Barack Obama, han invitado a George a la Casa Blanca.

George enjoys spending time with his daughter, Mayan. Sometimes he takes her to his special events. Other times, the special event is for Mayan. On her fifteenth birthday, he and Ann took her to Disneyland.

A George le gusta pasar tiempo con su hija Mayan. A veces la lleva a los eventos que asiste. Otras, el evento se hace especialmente para Mayan. Cuando cumplió quince años, George y Ann la llevaron a Disneyland.

23

In his free time, George likes to watch basketball, baseball, and other sports. When he was younger, he played Little League baseball.

En su tiempo libre, a George le gusta mirar baloncesto, béisbol y otros deportes. Cuando era pequeño, jugaba en las Ligas Pequeñas de béisbol.

George cheers for the Los Angeles Lakers basketball team.

George vitorea a los Lakers, el equipo de baloncesto de Los Ángeles.

George loves to play golf. He likes playing golf for charity even better. At Justin Timberlake's golf championship, he helped raise money for children's hospitals. George holds his own charity golf tournament each year, the George Lopez Celebrity Golf Classic.

A George le encanta jugar golf. Y todavía más si es para una organización benéfica. En el campeonato de golf de Justin Timberlake, George ayudó a recaudar dinero para los hospitales de niños. George celebra su propio campeonato de golf todos los años, el Clásico de Golf de Celebridades de George López.

¿Por Qué Lloras?

UNA MIRADA EN SERIO A LA VIDA, AL AMOR, Y LA RISA

GEORGE LÓPEZ

con Armen Keteyian

George wrote a book that was published in Spanish and in English. He stays busy making people laugh and making the world a better place, but he always takes time to talk to his fans. They all seem to want to know, "What's it like to be George López?"

George escribió un libro que se publicó en español e inglés. Se ocupa de hacer reír a la gente y de que el mundo sea un lugar mejor. Pero siempre dedica un tiempo a hablar con sus admiradores. Al parecer, todo lo que ellos quieren saber es "¿Qué se siente al ser George López?".

28

GEORGE LÓPEZ SELECTED WORKS
OBRAS SELECTAS DE GEORGE LÓPEZ

2011	*The Smurfs*
	Rio
	Beverly Hills Chihuahua 2 (Video)
2010	*Marmaduke*
	Valentine's Day
	Lopez Tonight (TV series)
	The Spy Next Door
2009	*Mr. Troop Mom* (TV movie)
2008	*Beverly Hills Chihuahua*
	Swing Vote
	Henry Poole Is Here
2007	*Balls of Fury*
	Tortilla Heaven
2005	*The Adventures of Sharkboy and Lavagirl 3-D*
2004	*Naughty or Nice* (TV movie)
2002 – 2007	*The George Lopez Show* (TV series)
2002	*Frank McKlusky, C.I.*
	Outta Time
	Fidel (TV movie)
	Real Women Have Curves
2000	*Bread and Roses*
1993	*Fatal Instinct*
1990	*Ski Patrol*

FURTHER READING
LECTURAS RECOMENDADAS

Books / Libros

Guzmán, Lila, and Rick Guzmán. *George Lopez: Latino King of Comedy*. Berkeley Heights, NJ: Enslow Publishers, 2009.

Guzmán, Lila, and Rick Guzmán. *George Lopez: Comediante y Estrella de TV*. Berkeley Heights, NJ: Enslow Publishers, 2009.

On the Internet / En Internet

George Lopez: Kids Corner
http://www.georgelopez.com/#/KidsCorner

Movie: *Beverly Hills Chihuahua*
http://disneydvd.disney.go.com/beverly-hills-chihuahua.html

Movie: *The Smurfs 3-D*
http://www.smurfhappens.com/

Nick at Night: *George Lopez Show*
http://www.nickatnite.com/shows/george-lopez/

PBS Documentary Information: Brown Is the New Green
http://www.brownisthenewgreen.net/

Works Consulted / Obras consultadas

George Lopez—Official Site
http://www.georgelopez.com/

George Lopez – The Complete First and Second Seasons. DVD. 2002.

Hispanic Culture Online: George Lopez
http://www.hispanic-culture-online.com/george-lopez-biography.html

IMDB: George Lopez
http://www.imdb.com/name/nm0520064/

Lopez, George, and Armen Keteyian. *Why You Crying? My Long, Hard Look at Life, Love, and Laughter*. New York: Simon & Schuster, 2004.

Lopez, George. *La comida y los ejercicios cuentan: creando hijos saludables y activos*. DVD. Washington, D.C.: Parents Action for Children, 2006.

Lopez Foundation
http://thelopezfoundation.org/

Lopez Tonight
http://lopeztonight.com/

INDEX/ÍNDICE

ABOUT THE AUTHOR: Karen Bush Gibson has written more than 30 educational books about famous people, different cultures, and historical events. She has written about Barack Obama, Adrian Peterson, and Jennifer López. She lives in Oklahoma, with her family, who all enjoy *The George Lopez Show*.

ACERCA DE LA AUTORA: Karen Bush Gibson ha escrito más de 30 libros educacionales sobre gente famosa, culturas diferentes y acontecimientos históricos. Ha escrito sobre Barack Obama, Adrian Peterson y Jennifer López. Vive con su familia en Oklahoma, y todos disfrutan *The George Lopez Show*.

ABOUT THE TRANSLATOR: Eida de la Vega was born in Havana, Cuba, and now lives in New Jersey with her mother, her husband, and her two children. Eida has worked at Lectorum/Scholastic, and as editor of the magazine *Selecciones del Reader's Digest*.

ACERCA DE LA TRADUCTORA: Eida de la Vega nació en La Habana, Cuba, y ahora vive en Nueva Jersey con su madre, su esposo y sus dos hijos. Ha trabajado en Lectorum/Scholastic y, como editora, en la revista *Selecciones del Reader's Digest*.